GODS & GODDESSES

OF THE ANCIENT

Ma'at

BY VIRGINIA LOH-HAGAN

Gods and goddesses were the main characters of myths. Myths are traditional stories from ancient cultures. Storytellers answered questions about the world by creating exciting explanations. People thought myths were true. Myths explained the unexplainable. They helped people make sense of human behavior and nature. Today, we use science to explain the world. But people still love myths. Myths may not be literally true. But they have meaning. They tell us something about our history and culture.

45th Parallel Press

Published in the United States of America by Cherry Lake Publishing
Ann Arbor, Michigan
www.cherrylakepublishing.com

Reading Adviser: Marla Conn, MS, Ed., Literacy specialist, Read-Ability, Inc.
Book Design: Jen Wahi

Photo Credits: ©Howard David Johnson, 2019, cover, 1, 25; ©SHIK_SHIK/Shutterstock, 5; ©amelipulen/Shutterstock, 6;
©Erhan Dayi/Dreamstime, 9; ©Andrea Izzotti/Shutterstock, 11; ©francesco de marco/Shutterstock, 13; ©givaga/Shutterstock, 14;
Leon Jean Joseph Dubois (1780–1846)/rawpixel/Public domain, 17; ©Paolo Gallo/Shutterstock, 18; ©Snova/Shutterstock, 21;
©Petr Bonek/Shutterstock, 22; ©oner Nguyen/Shutterstock, 26; ©Emotionart/Dreamstime, 28

45th Parallel Press is an imprint of Cherry Lake Publishing.

Library of Congress Cataloging-in-Publication Data

Names: Loh-Hagan, Virginia, author. | Loh-Hagan, Virginia. Gods & goddesses of the ancient world.
Title: Ma'at / written by Virginia Loh-Hagan.
Description: Ann Arbor, Michigan : Cherry Lake Publishing, 2019. | Series: Gods and goddesses of the ancient world
Identifiers: LCCN 2019004233 | ISBN 9781534147782 (hardcover) | ISBN 9781534149212 (pdf) | ISBN 9781534150645 (pbk.) |
   ISBN 9781534152076 (hosted ebook)
Subjects: LCSH: Maat (Egyptian deity)—Juvenile literature. | Goddesses, Egyptian—Juvenile literature. | Mythology, Egyptian—
   Juvenile literature.
Classification: LCC BL2450.M33 L64 2019 | DDC 299/.312114—dc23
LC record available at https://lccn.loc.gov/2019004233

Printed in the United States of America
Corporate Graphics

ABOUT THE AUTHOR:

Dr. Virginia Loh-Hagan is an author, university professor, former classroom teacher,
and curriculum designer. She doesn't like to be weighed. She avoids scales. She lives in
San Diego with her very tall husband and very naughty dogs. To learn more about her,
visit www.virginialoh.com.

TABLE OF CONTENTS

CHAPTER 1

NOTHING BUT THE TRUTH

Who is Ma'at? What does she look like? What does she do?

Ma'at was an **ancient** Egyptian goddess. Ancient means old. Egypt is a country in the Middle East. It's in North Africa.

Ancient Egyptians honored Ma'at. Ma'at was a young woman. She was tall. She wore a white dress. She wore a lot of jewelry. She had wings on each arm. She wore an **ostrich** feather in her hair. An ostrich is a big bird. It doesn't fly. An ostrich feather is the symbol for truth.

Ma'at held a **scepter**. Scepters are poles. They have fancy designs. They're a symbol of power. Ma'at also holds an **ankh**. An ankh is shaped like a cross with an open top. It represents eternal life. Eternal means forever.

 Ma'at is usually shown with open arms.

Ma'at didn't like change. She liked tradition.

Ma'at was the goddess of truth. She was the goddess of justice. She was the goddess of law and order. She was the goddess of balance and harmony. She balanced the stars. She controlled the seasons. She put together the universe, nature, government, and people. She put everything in order.

Ma'at managed human actions. She gave humans rules to live a good life. Ancient Egyptians lived life according to Ma'at. They acted with honor. They told the truth. They had to be fair. They were loyal. If not, they were punished.

Ma'at helped pharaohs. Pharaohs were ancient Egyptian kings. They called themselves the "lords of Ma'at."

Family Tree

Grandparent: Nun (water of disorder)

Parent: Ra (Sun God)

Siblings: Shu (god of light and dry air), Tefnut (goddess of wet air and rain), Hathor (goddess of sky, women, fertility, and love), Sekhmet (goddess of healing), and Bastet (goddess of ointment, home, cats, and women's secrets)

Husband: Thoth (god of writing, magic, wisdom, and moon)

Children: gods of Hermopolis

They "presented Ma'at" to the gods. They did this when they took over the throne. They ruled by Ma'at's laws. They saved and defended Ma'at.

Ma'at helped lawyers and judges. Ancient Egyptian lawyers and judges had a special name. They were called "priests of Ma'at." They worked for Ma'at. They defended the weak. They defended the poor. They put green dye on their tongues. This meant their words were true. Judges wore ostrich feathers when they started court. The winner got the feather. The loser got punished.

Ancient Egyptians who worked in law wore a pin with Ma'at's picture.

CHAPTER 2

TIPPING THE SCALES

Who is Anubis? What does Ma'at do in the Hall of Truth?

Ancient Egyptians wanted to live a good life. They wanted to have a good **afterlife**. Afterlife is life after death. To have a good afterlife, ancient Egyptians had to worship Ma'at. They had to know right from wrong. They didn't have to be perfect. But they had to have balance. They needed to do more good things than bad things.

Ancient Egyptians died. Their bodies got **embalmed**. Anubis was the god of embalming. Embalming is the

preserving of human bodies after dying. Preserving means saving. Embalmers took out body parts. They put special chemicals in bodies. This process kept bodies from rotting.

Ancient Egyptians made mummies.

All in the Family

Ancient Egyptians loved cats. Cats hunted mice and snakes. These pests destroyed their farms. Egyptians thought cats were Bastet's spirit. In one of Bastet's temples, over 300,000 mummy cats were found. Bastet had a woman's body. She had a cat's head. Sometimes, she was a lion. She was an ancient Egyptian goddess. She was the goddess of ointment. Ointments are healing creams. They're also perfumes. Bastet was the goddess of homes. She protected all homes. She protected people from getting sick. She protected people from evil spirits. She helped women have many babies. She worked in the underworld. She helped prepare dead bodies. She also kept people's secrets. She took their secrets to the grave. In some stories, she was married to Anubis. Anubis was the god of embalming. In other stories, she was married to Ptah. Ptah was the god of builders.

Hearts were left in Egyptian mummies while their other organs were removed.

Ancient Egyptians' souls took a journey to the **underworld**. The underworld was the place where dead souls lived. This happened while their bodies were getting embalmed. Anubis led souls to the **Hall** of Truth. Hall means house or great room. Ma'at lived in the Hall of Truth. Souls lined up. They waited to be judged. Anubis and Ma'at were the judges.

Anubis and Ma'at decided if souls were worthy or not. Anubis took the heart. Hearts were people's souls. Anubis put hearts on a **scale**. Scales are tools. They measure things.

They represent balance. Anubis measured it against Ma'at. Ma'at appeared as a feather. She helped weigh the hearts.

Each soul had to say Ma'at's 42 Truths. An example is "I have not lied."

Souls heavier than a feather were given to Ammut. Ammut was a monster. She was known as the "eater of hearts." She ate the hearts of bad souls. These souls didn't live life by Ma'at's rules. They died 2 deaths. They were restless forever.

Souls lighter than a feather could go to the afterlife. Light souls were good. These souls followed Ma'at's rules. They could have an eternal life. They could go to the "Fields of **Reeds**." Reeds are grasses. This was a magical place like heaven.

 Ma'at helped the ancient Egyptians make good choices.

CHAPTER 3

TOOLS OF TRUTH

What are Ma'at's symbols? What tools help Ma'at?

Ostrich feathers are Ma'at's main symbol. Ma'at wore one single feather. Ancient Egyptians honored ostriches. Ostriches were a symbol of creation and light. Their feathers are special. They are **symmetrical**. This means the hairs on each side of the stem are the same size. As such, they represented fairness and balance.

Ostriches are the largest and heaviest birds. They're too heavy to fly. But they still use their wings. They hold their wings out for balance. They need balance to run. They run fast. They use their feathers to communicate. To show power, they lift their feathers up. To show **submission**, their feathers droop down. Submission means to obey.

In ancient Egyptian art, ostrich feathers were shown with a curled top, like pictured here.

There are over 190 chapters in the Book of the Dead.

One of Ma'at's tools was the Book of the Dead. This book is a collection. It has instructions. It helped people through the underworld. It lists Ma'at's 42 Truths.

Ma'at had 42 judges who helped her. The judges represented each truth. They represented a part of Ma'at. They were the godly beings of the Egyptian afterlife. They lived in the Hall of Truth.

Before being weighed by Ma'at, souls **confessed**. Confess means to admit. They shared their sins. They declared their **innocence**. Innocence means not being guilty.

Real World Connection

Like Ma'at, Ruth Bader Ginsburg is a judge. Ginsburg was born in 1933. She was born in New York. She's a U.S. Supreme Court justice. She rules in the highest court of the land. She studied law at top law schools. She was top of her class. She taught in law schools. She fought for women's rights. She fought for the rights of workers. She wasn't always treated fairly. It was because she was a woman. She said, "Not a law firm in the entire city of New York would employ me. I struck out on three grounds: I was Jewish, a woman, and a mother." She's known as Notorious R.B.G. Notorious means famous. She's famous for saying, "I dissent." Dissent means to disagree. She's not afraid to fight for her causes.

CHAPTER 4

A BALANCED LIFE

Who is Thoth? Who is Isfet?

Ma'at had 2 people who balanced her life. Thoth was her husband. Isfet was her enemy.

Thoth was the god of wisdom. He was the god of magic. He was the god of writing. He was the god of the moon. He helped end fights between gods. He taught humans how to write. He helped Ma'at judge the dead.

Thoth and Ma'at were a good couple. They represented truth and wisdom. Together, they make good decisions. In some stories, they had 8 children. The children were gods of Hermopolis. Hermopolis was an ancient Egyptian city. Ancient Egyptians believed the world was both good and bad. They thought the world was always fighting between order and disorder. Ma'at and Isfet kept these forces in balance.

In Greek myths, Thoth was Hermes.

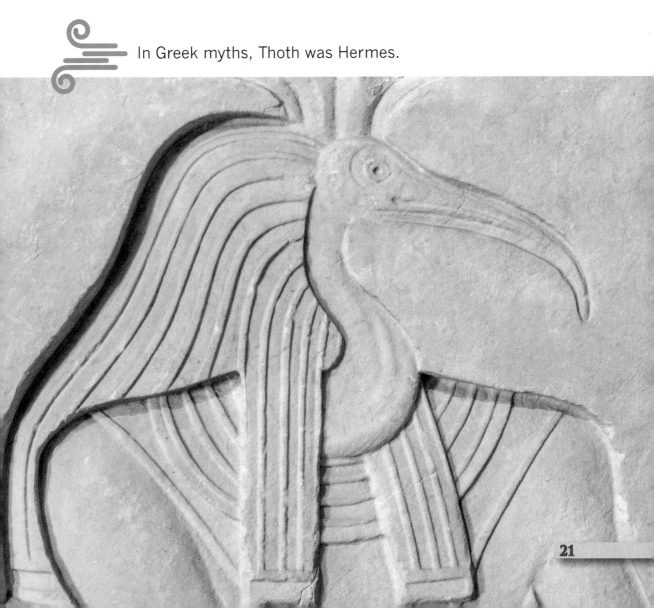

Pharaohs had to please Ma'at.

Isfet was Ma'at's opposite. She was the goddess of disorder. She caused violence. She caused evil. She made things unfair. Ma'at and Isfet balanced each other. They needed each other. Without Isfet, there'd be no Ma'at. Ma'at had to overcome Isfet. Isfet had to beat Ma'at.

Pharaohs had to "achieve Ma'at." This means they had to protect justice by destroying Isfet. If there was peace, Ma'at was in control. If there was war, Isfet was in control.

Cross-Cultural Connection

Like Ma'at, Meng Po worked with the dead. She was a Chinese goddess. She was the goddess of forgetfulness. Forgetfulness means to not remember. Meng Po looked like an old woman. Sometimes, she was called Old Lady Meng. Meng Po lived in the Chinese realm of the dead. This is like the underworld. She worked with dead people's souls. These souls wanted to be reincarnated. This means they wanted to be born again with a new life. Meng Po's job was to make sure souls forgot about their previous lives. She made a special tea. She used special herbs. She used magical pond water. The tea had magic. It made people lose their memories. It got rid of their sins. It got rid of their knowledge. Meng Po made souls drink it. She wouldn't let them return to earth until they drank it. She prepared them for their next lives.

CHAPTER 5

RISING TO THE TOP

What are some stories about Ma'at? How is Ma'at born? How does she help Ra?

In the beginning, the world was crazy. There was no order. Nun was the first waters. He was the water of **chaos**. Chaos means disorder. Ra was the Sun God. He created himself from Nun's waters. He emerged as a mound of dirt. Sunlight hit the mound. It gave the dirt power. Ra came up from the waters. He rose. The dirt became Ra.

Ma'at is considered a creator goddess.

In stories, Ma'at's and Ra's boat was called "day bark" and "night bark."

Heka was the god of magic. He was the god of medicine. He used his magic to make Ma'at. Ma'at was born when Ra rose from Nun. This made Ra her father.

Explained By Science

Adult hearts are the size of closed fists. A man's heart weighs about 10 ounces (283 grams). A woman's heart weighs about 8 ounces (227 g). The heart is a strong muscle. It pumps in and out. It pumps 2,000 gallons (7,571 liters) of blood a day. It has 4 chambers. Chambers are like rooms. The top chambers are called atria. They pump in blood from the body and lungs. They fill with blood. They dump it into the bottom chambers. The bottom chambers are called ventricles. They squeeze. They pump out blood to the body and lungs. While the ventricles are squeezing, the atria are filling up again. The heart has valves. Valves are like doors. They keep the blood flowing forward. They open to let blood move ahead. They close quickly to keep blood from flowing back in. Blood sends oxygen to all the body's cells. Cells would die without oxygen. People would die without living cells.

In some stories, Ma'at gave gods the power to breathe.

Ma'at also helped Ra in other ways. Ra lived in the sky. He had a special boat. His boat was called "the boat of millions of years." Ra sailed across the sky. He did this every day. Ma'at stood at the front of his boat. She helped Ra control the sun's movement.

In the morning, they sailed from the east. As they sailed, the sun rose. They sailed the boat toward the west. As they sailed, the sun went down. At night, they sailed into the underworld. This was where Ma'at weighed hearts.

Ra's main enemy was Apep. Apep was an evil snake. He was the lord of chaos. He was the bringer of darkness. Ra was the bringer of light.

Apep tried to stop Ra's boat. He did this every day. Ra fought him every day. He did this as he sailed. Sometimes, Ra turned into a cat. He attacked Apep. Sunny days meant Ra won. Stormy days meant Apep won.

Ma'at helped Ra. She made sure Apep didn't take over. She balanced light and dark.

Don't anger the goddesses. Ma'at had great powers. And she knew how to use them.

- Ma'at's name means "that which is the truth." Sometimes, she's called Ma'at. Sometimes, she's called Mayet. Ma'at is a popular name in Egypt and Africa.

- Karnak is a village in Egypt. It has a lot of historical buildings. It has a Ma'at temple. Temples are places of worship. The Ma'at temple was used as a court. People met to talk about crimes. The biggest crime was the robbing of royal tombs. Tombs are places where pharaohs were buried.

- A plinth is a heavy base. It supports a statue or vase. Ancient Egyptians wrote Ma'at's name on plinths with her statues. They didn't usually do this for other gods or goddesses. This means that Ma'at was special. Ma'at was the foundation of Egyptian society.

- There are stories of Ma'at as a ruler. This time was called a Golden Age. Ma'at ruled over humans. She saw how evil people could be. This made her sad. Ma'at went back to the heavens.

- Some Egyptians say, "I'll be joining Ma'at." This means they're dying. People think of Ma'at as a guardian angel.

- Hatshepsut was an ancient Egyptian pharaoh. She ruled from 1478 to 1458 BCE. She was one of the few female pharaohs. She called herself Ma'atkare. Ma'at means "truth." Ka means "soul." And Re means "sun god." Hatshepsut thought this name would give her more power. She wanted the people to respect her.

CONSIDER THIS!

TAKE A POSITION! Egyptian law was based on Ma'at. Law and order are important. Read the 45th Parallel Press book about Ra. Ra was a creator god. Who is more important: Ra or Ma'at? Why do you think so? Argue your point with reasons and evidence.

SAY WHAT? Anubis and Ma'at work together. How are they connected? What do they do? Explain their jobs. Explain what happens in the underworld. Draw a map. List the steps.

THINK ABOUT IT! Ma'at and Isfet are opposites. Ma'at is order. Isfet is disorder. Ma'at and Isfet balance each other. Is there someone who balances you? Is there someone who's the opposite of you? How so?

LEARN MORE

Braun, Eric. *Egyptian Myths.* North Mankato, MN: Capstone Press, 2019.

Napoli, Donna Jo, and Christina Balit (illust.). *Treasury of Egyptian Mythology: Classic Stories of Gods, Goddesses, Monsters, and Mortals.* Washington, DC: National Geographic Kids, 2013.

Reinhart, Matthew, and Robert Sabuda. *Gods and Heroes.* Somerville, MA: Candlewick Press, 2010.

GLOSSARY

afterlife (AF-tur-life) life after death

ancient (AYN-shuhnt) old, from a long time ago

ankh (ANK) an object with a loop used in ancient Egypt as a symbol of life

chaos (KAY-ahs) disorder

confessed (kuhn-FESD) admitted something bad

embalmed (em-BAHMD) preserved by treating human remains with chemicals to keep bodies from rotting

hall (HAWL) house or great room

innocence (IN-uh-suhns) not being guilty

ostrich (AWS-trich) a large, flightless bird

preserving (prih-ZURV-ing) saving over time

reeds (REEDZ) tall grasses

scale (SKAYL) tool used to measure things

scepter (SEP-tur) a large staff or pole that is decorated and used to show power or authority

submission (suhb-MISH-uhn) obedience

symmetrical (sih-MET-rih-kuhl) a balanced arrangement of parts on either side of a line

underworld (UHN-dur-wurld) the land of the dead

INDEX